Rita Rudner's Guide to Men

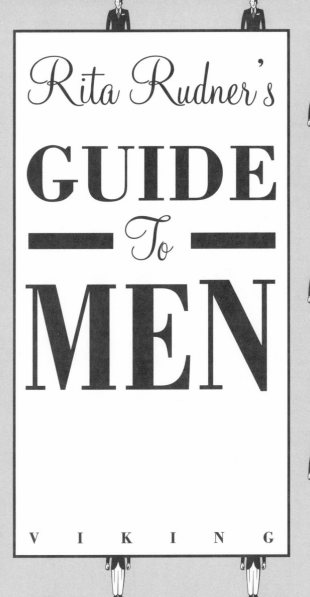

Rita Rudner's
GUIDE
To
MEN

V I K I N G

VIKING
Published by the Penguin Group
Penguin Books USA Inc., 375 Hudson Street,
New York, New York 10014, U.S.A.
Penguin Books Ltd, 27 Wrights Lane, London W8 5TZ, England
Penguin Books Australia Ltd, Ringwood, Victoria, Australia
Penguin Books Canada Ltd, 10 Alcorn Avenue,
Toronto, Ontario, Canada M4V 3B2
Penguin Books (N.Z.) Ltd, 182–190 Wairau Road,
Auckland 10, New Zealand

Penguin Books Ltd, Registered Offices:
Harmondsworth, Middlesex, England

First published in 1994 by Viking Penguin,
a division of Penguin Books USA Inc.

1 3 5 7 9 10 8 6 4 2

Copyright © Rita Rudner Enterprises, Inc., 1994
Illustrations copyright © Viking Penguin,
a division of Penguin Books, USA Inc., 1994
All rights reserved

ISBN 0-670-85507-3
Library of Congress Cataloging-in-Publication Data available

Printed in the United States of America
Set in Bodoni and Monterey

DESIGNED BY BRIAN MULLIGAN
INTERIOR ILLUSTRATIONS BY ROBERT CLYDE ANDERSON

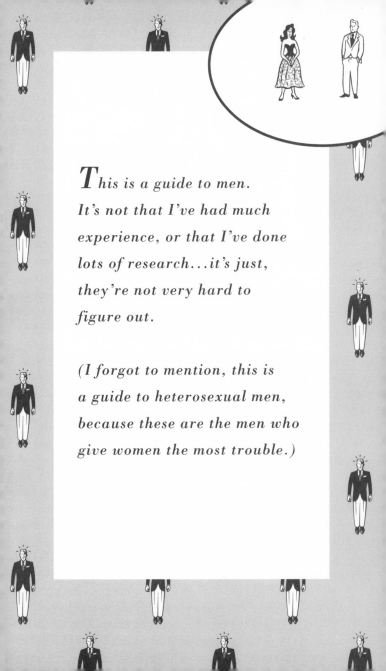

*T*his is a guide to men.
It's not that I've had much
experience, or that I've done
lots of research...it's just,
they're not very hard to
figure out.

*(I forgot to mention, this is
a guide to heterosexual men,
because these are the men who
give women the most trouble.)*

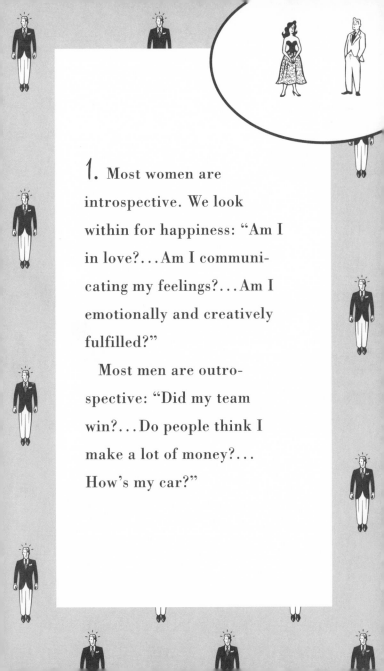

1. Most women are introspective. We look within for happiness: "Am I in love?...Am I communicating my feelings?...Am I emotionally and creatively fulfilled?"

Most men are outrospective: "Did my team win?...Do people think I make a lot of money?... How's my car?"

Rita Rudner's

2. The way a man plays a game can be very revealing. I was playing tennis with a man I had been dating for a while and noticed his reluctance to keep score properly. He couldn't say, "Thirty-love." He kept saying, "Thirty, I really like you but I still have to see other people."

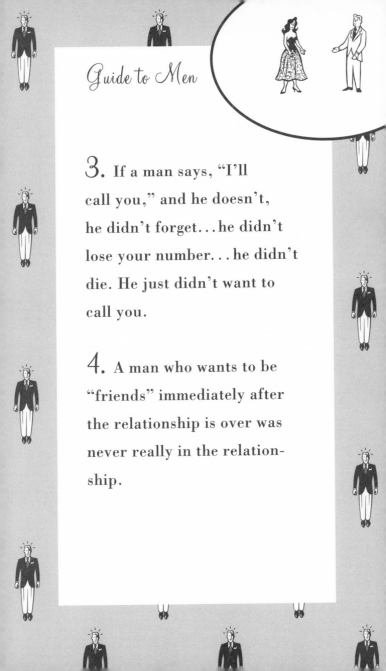

3. If a man says, "I'll call you," and he doesn't, he didn't forget... he didn't lose your number... he didn't die. He just didn't want to call you.

4. A man who wants to be "friends" immediately after the relationship is over was never really in the relationship.

Rita Rudner's

5. Men who fought in World War One are now either very old or dead.

6. Most of the men sitting in first class on an airplane have really boring jobs.

7. Most men who hitchhike have never sat in first class on an airplane.

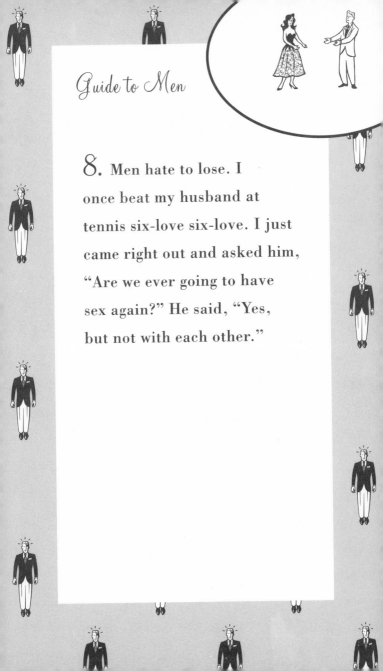

8. Men hate to lose. I once beat my husband at tennis six-love six-love. I just came right out and asked him, "Are we ever going to have sex again?" He said, "Yes, but not with each other."

9. Men who can eat anything they want and not gain weight should do it out of sight of the women they're married to.

10. A man's medicine cabinet will tell you everything you need to know about him.

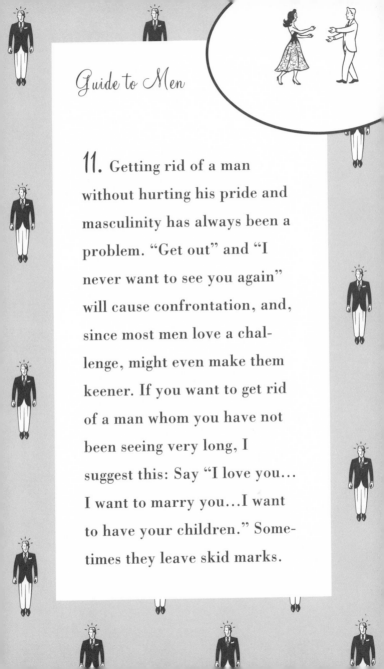

Guide to Men

11. Getting rid of a man without hurting his pride and masculinity has always been a problem. "Get out" and "I never want to see you again" will cause confrontation, and, since most men love a challenge, might even make them keener. If you want to get rid of a man whom you have not been seeing very long, I suggest this: Say "I love you... I want to marry you...I want to have your children." Sometimes they leave skid marks.

12. If you buy your husband or boyfriend a video camera, for the first few weeks he has it, lock the door when you go to the bathroom. For some reason they think surprising you in the bathroom is hysterical. Most of my husband's early films end with a scream and a flush.

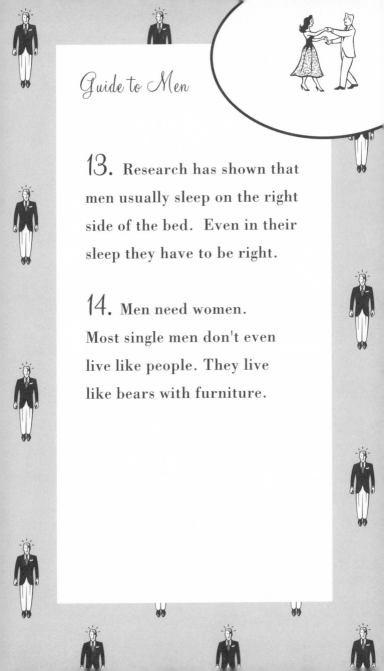

13. Research has shown that men usually sleep on the right side of the bed. Even in their sleep they have to be right.

14. Men need women. Most single men don't even live like people. They live like bears with furniture.

Rita Rudner's

15. Bald men are often
nicer than men with hair. Lots
of women don't want to date
bald men, so they are aware
that they appeal to a limited
market. Be careful of men
who are bald and rich; the
arrogance of "rich" usually
cancels out the nice of "bald"
and you might as well shoot
for someone with hair.

Guide to Men

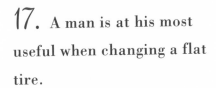

16. Men who work out all the time are very tired. Marathon runners, triathloners, and men who ride bikes up mountains will just manage a kiss good-night before rolling over and falling into a stupor.

17. A man is at his most useful when changing a flat tire.

18. All men hate verbal confrontation. "We need to talk about our relationship" strikes fear in the heart of even General Schwarzkopf.

Guide to Men

19. Men don't understand comfortable dressing for women. We'll be going out to dinner and my husband will say, "Please, don't make me wear a tie, I can't breathe, I can't swallow, don't make me wear a tie." I say, "Okay, don't wear a tie. What should I wear?" He says, "How about that iron bustier with the torture lacing?"

Rita Rudner's

20. Most men are very difficult to buy presents for. Last year I gave up and handed my father a hundred dollars and said, "Just buy yourself something that will make your life easier." He went out and bought a present for my mother.

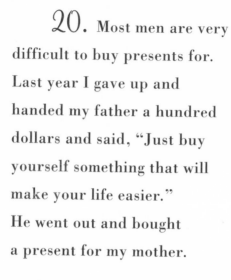

Guide to Men

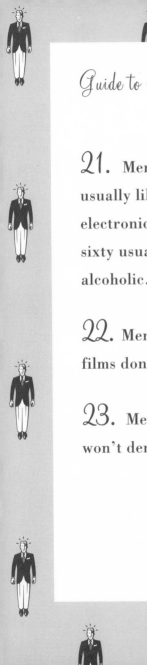

21. Men under sixty usually like anything electronic. Men over sixty usually like anything alcoholic.

22. Men who like foreign films don't eat at Denny's.

23. Men who eat at Denny's won't demand a prenuptial.

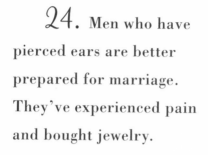

24. Men who have pierced ears are better prepared for marriage. They've experienced pain and bought jewelry.

25. Men love to conquer nature without exerting effort. All men would love to own a lawn mower that they can ride.

Guide to Men

26. Always check out a man's pets before getting too involved. Dogs, cats, fish...fine. Snakes, bats, rats...run.

27. Marrying a man who has been married before is ecologically responsible. In a world where there are more women than men it makes sense to recycle.

28. Men are very confident people. My husband is so confident that when he watches sports on television, he thinks that if he concentrates he can help his team. If they're in trouble, he coaches them from our living room, and if they're really in trouble I have to get off the phone in case they call him.

Guide to Men

29. If it's attention you want, don't get involved with any man during play-off season.

30. Men like phones with lots of buttons. It makes them feel important.

31. Men love to be the first to read the newspaper in the morning. Even if a paper is refolded immaculately, the fact that they have not been the first is upsetting to their psyches.

Rita Rudner's

32. All men look handsome in a navy blue suit.

33. All men look nerdy in black socks and sandals.

34. All men look racist in Ku Klux Klan outfits.

35. The way a man looks at himself in a mirror will tell you if he can ever care about anyone else.

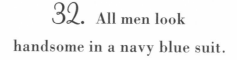

Guide to Men

36. Men have better self-images than women. You know what I've never seen in a men's magazine? A makeover.

37. Men secretly borrow women's cover-up sticks. For a little gift get them their own. I recommend Maybelline.

Rita Rudner's

38. Don't try to teach a man how to do anything in public. They can learn in private; in public they have to know.

39. Men who are not going bald seldom wear baseball caps.

40. Men who have prominent chins seldom grow beards.

41. All men are afraid of eyelash curlers. They don't understand them, and they don't want to get near them. I sleep with one under my pillow, instead of a gun.

42. A good place to meet a man is at the dry cleaner's. These men usually have jobs and are hygienically responsible.

43. If you like easygoing, monogamous men, stay away from billionaires.

44. Rich men are often the stingiest. I had one rich boyfriend. When we went out to dinner, I used to order lobster just to watch his pupils constrict.

45. Men love watches that have multiple functions. My husband has one that is a combination address book, telescope, and piano.

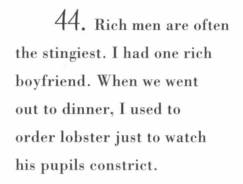

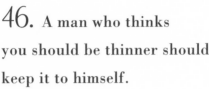

Guide to Men

46. A man who thinks you should be thinner should keep it to himself.

47. Men who tell you they read the "Victoria's Secret" catalogue for the articles are lying.

48. Men love the remote control. A man who gives up possession of it is probably a man who is looking at the "Victoria's Secret" catalogue.

49. Men do not think ahead. Example: A woman going to the movies in the summer thinks, "It's hot out but I'm going to the movies and it might be over–air-conditioned, I'll take a sweater." Result: She is prepared.

A man going to the movies thinks, "It's hot out. I'm in my shorts and T-shirt, let's roll." Result: He gets pneumonia. (The really strange thing is that the man would rather get pneumonia than bring a sweater.)

Guide to Men

50. Men who have
been to prison will usually
get up very early.

51. A man who shaves
more than three times a day
should not become a female
impersonator.

52. Men who maintain their
fish tanks have some sense of
responsibility.

53. Men's old T-shirts make
excellent women's pajamas.

Rita Rudner's

54. Men are sensitive in strange ways. If a man has built a fire and the last bit of wood does not burn...he will take it personally.

55. Men do not like to admit to even momentary imperfection. My husband forgot the code to turn off our burglar alarm. When the police came, he wouldn't admit he'd forgotten the code...he turned himself in.

Guide to Men

56. Older men are not more mature. They just have more money...which makes them appear more mature.

57. All men would still really like to own a train set.

58. Men who consistently leave the toilet seat up secretly want women to get up to go to the bathroom in the middle of the night and fall in.

59. Morning deejays have to get up very, very early. Men who have been to prison make good morning deejays.

60. Men like cars, women like clothes. Women only like cars because they take them to clothes.

61. Men don't like to talk on the phone unless they have something specific to say.

Guide to Men

62. Men won't go shopping unless they need something.

63. Men are brave enough to go to war, but they are not brave enough to get a bikini wax.

64. All men think that they're nice guys. Some of them are not. Contact me for a list of names.

65. Single men's apartments never smell good.

66. Men don't get cellulite. God might just be a man.

67. Men have an easier time buying bathing suits. Women have two types: depressing and more depressing. Men have two types: nerdy and not nerdy.

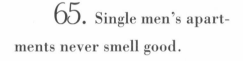

Guide to Men

68. Men have higher body temperatures than women. If your heating goes out in the winter, I recommend sleeping next to a man. Men are like portable heaters that snore.

69. Men who drink herbal teas are seldom serial killers.

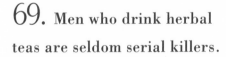

Rita Rudner's

70. Men are very impatient. They need to drive faster and get places quicker. Maybe that's because they die younger...or maybe they die younger because they need to drive faster and get places quicker.

71. A man who continually takes vacations by himself is hiding something.

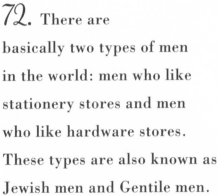

Guide to Men

72. There are
basically two types of men
in the world: men who like
stationery stores and men
who like hardware stores.
These types are also known as
Jewish men and Gentile men.

73. Men who write love
letters don't live in this
century.

Rita Rudner's

74. Women take clothing much more seriously than men. I've never seen a man walk into a party and say, "Oh my God, I'm so embarrassed; get me out of here, there's another man wearing a black tuxedo." They're happy—if they all look alike it means they haven't made a mistake.

Guide to Men

75. Most men hate to shop. That's why in department stores the men's department is usually on the first floor, two inches from the door.

76. Men do cry, but only when assembling furniture from Ikea.

77. If a man prepares dinner for you and the salad contains three or more types of lettuce, he is serious about the relationship.

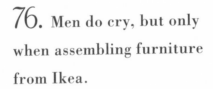

78. Men who go on "Jeopardy" seldom get asked to pose nude.

79. Male tennis players wear more jewelry than male ballet dancers.

80. A starving artist marrying a rich woman will not demand a prenuptial.

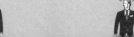

Guide to Men

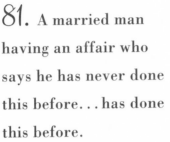

81. A married man having an affair who says he has never done this before... has done this before.

82. Whatever it was that Mike Tyson did... he won't do it again.

83. Investment bankers don't get the movie *Spinal Tap*.

84. Professional bowlers don't wear Armani.

Rita Rudner's

85. The weather changes, people do not. If you're dating a man who you think might be "Mr. Right" if he a) got older, b) got a new job, or c) started going to a psychiatrist, you are going to get a nasty surprise. The cocoon-to-butterfly theory only works on cocoons and butterflies. (A near-death experience sometimes changes people, but even this is usually temporary.)

Guide to Men

86. Men are much more likely than women to weigh themselves in public.

87. Stay away from men who wear devil-worship rings on their index fingers.

88. Men who drive trucks that have curvaceous women carved into their mud flaps have never read *The Female Eunuch*.

89. Men who get their shoes shined more than twice a week are spending too much time on their feet.

90. If you're in a car with a man and he stops and asks someone for directions, listen carefully, because he won't, and it will be your fault if you get lost.

91. Men who live in glass houses shouldn't walk around naked.

92. Rock stars marry models.

93. Comedians want to marry models.

94. Models want to marry rock stars.

95. Non-gorgeous men with good personalities fare better than non-gorgeous women with good personalities. Julia Roberts married Lyle Lovett. Paulina Porizkova married Rick Ocasek. Elizabeth Taylor married Larry Fortensky. Mama Cass died single.

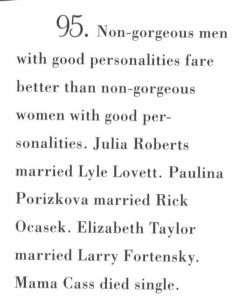

Guide to Men

96. Men own basket-
ball teams. Every year
cheerleaders' outfits get
tighter and briefer, and
professional basketball
players' shorts get baggier
and longer.

97. Sumo wrestlers have
trouble buying clothing.

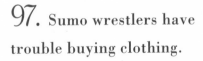

98. No man is charming all
of the time. Even Cary Grant
is on record saying he wished
he could be Cary Grant.

Rita Rudner's

99. A man who plays Frisbee with his dog in the park on a weekday afternoon makes under a hundred thousand dollars a year.

100. Men who buy a new car every year usually have trouble committing to a relationship.

Guide to Men

101. When four or
more men get together,
they talk about sports.

102. When four or more
women get together, they
talk about men.

Rita Rudner's

103. Not one man who drinks beer in a beer commercial has a beer belly.

104. Men are less sentimental than women. No man has ever seen the movie *The Way We Were* twice, voluntarily.

Guide to Men

105. Most men don't get "Oprah."

106. Men in high levels of government seldom surf.

107. International playboys have never eaten Spam.

108. Bullfighters probably don't bother with seat belts.

109. Men who only fall in love with blondes are called peroxosexuals.

110. Men who only fall in love with lesbians are called lesbosexuals.

111. Men who only fall in love with women who used to be men are called ex-penisexuals.

Guide to Men

112. Men who call the "Love Hotline" on a regular basis should not ask their friends to fix them up with a nice girl.

113. Men who stockpile semi-automatic weapons in their basements should be investigated.

114. Men who own high-powered telescopes usually aren't into astronomy.

Rita Rudner's

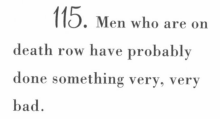

115. Men who are on death row have probably done something very, very bad.

116. Men will now get up and walk with the baby in the middle of the night, change its diapers and give it a bottle, but in their heart of hearts they still think they shouldn't have to.

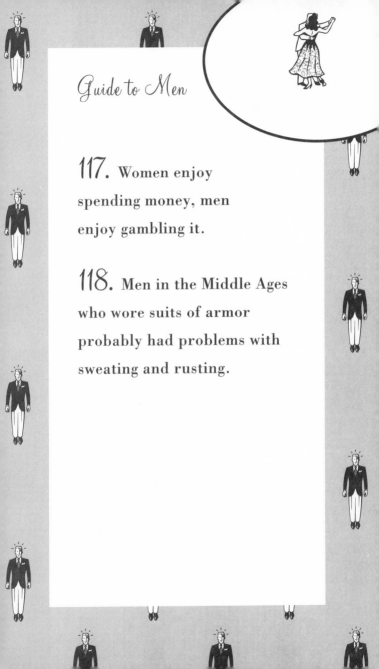

Guide to Men

117. Women enjoy spending money, men enjoy gambling it.

118. Men in the Middle Ages who wore suits of armor probably had problems with sweating and rusting.

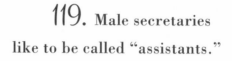

119. Male secretaries like to be called "assistants."

120. A man in a delivery room is about as helpful as a nun at a bar mitzvah.

121. Men who pull T-shirts over the backs of their car seats drink a lot of beer.

Guide to Men

122. Men name their children after themselves, women don't. Have you ever met a Sally, Jr.?

123. Men love to keep piles of change around in ashtrays.

124. As far as I know, a single man has never vacuumed behind a couch.

125. If you want a man to come dress-shopping with you, pick a store that has a chair. Sometimes my husband and I go into a store that has a chair, but there is already a comatose man sitting there. I always bring a folding chair for these situations.

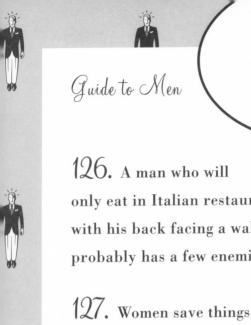

Guide to Men

126. A man who will only eat in Italian restaurants with his back facing a wall probably has a few enemies.

127. Women save things from their childhood, men don't. If a grown man has a collection of stuffed animals, he is a taxidermist.

128. Single men usually don't bother buying dust ruffles.

129. Women are more spiritual than men. There are no male fortune-tellers.

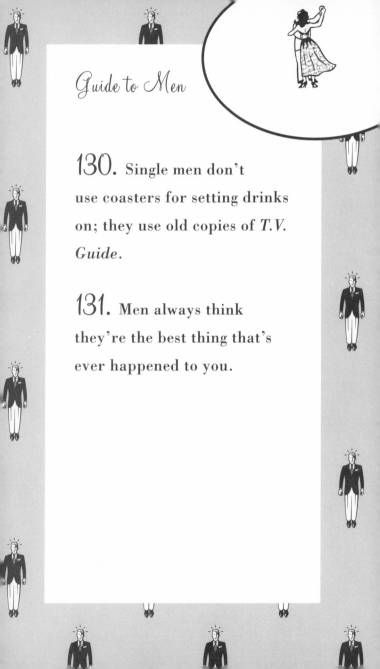

Guide to Men

130. Single men don't use coasters for setting drinks on; they use old copies of *T.V. Guide*.

131. Men always think they're the best thing that's ever happened to you.

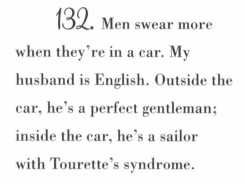

132. Men swear more when they're in a car. My husband is English. Outside the car, he's a perfect gentleman; inside the car, he's a sailor with Tourette's syndrome.

133. My husband will cook but not "cook, cook." He'll only barbecue. Men will cook as long as there is danger involved.

134. Men who use indoor tanning cream are a funny color.

Guide to Men

135. Men lie about their salaries, women lie about their age.

136. Men who really hunt don't wear Ralph Lauren's "Safari."

137. "Bellboys" over the age of thirty should be called "bellmen."

Rita Rudner's

138. Sexual rules have changed considerably. Single men who have had vasectomies to avoid wearing condoms probably feel pretty stupid and are now wearing condoms.

139. Men who drink vodka out of a paper bag have never been to the ballet.

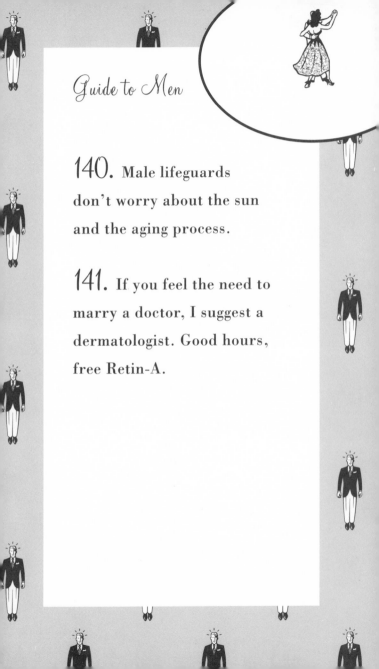

Guide to Men

140. Male lifeguards don't worry about the sun and the aging process.

141. If you feel the need to marry a doctor, I suggest a dermatologist. Good hours, free Retin-A.

142. Men accept compliments much better than women do. Example: "Mitch, you look great." Mitch: "Thank you." On the other side: "Ruth, you look great." Ruth: "I do? Maybe it's the lighting."

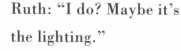

Guide to Men

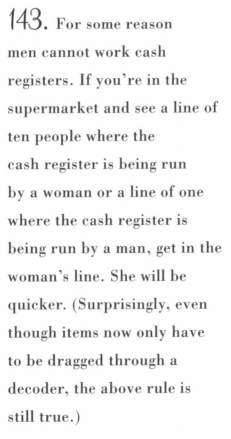

143. For some reason men cannot work cash registers. If you're in the supermarket and see a line of ten people where the cash register is being run by a woman or a line of one where the cash register is being run by a man, get in the woman's line. She will be quicker. (Surprisingly, even though items now only have to be dragged through a decoder, the above rule is still true.)

144. Most men are secretly still mad at their mothers for throwing away their comic books. They would be valuable now.

145. Men like camping more than women do because of the ease of their bathroom situation.

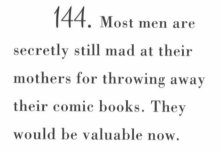

146. Men who aren't handy should have at least one friend who is.

Guide to Men

147. Men who listen to
classical music tend not
to spit.

148. Only men who have
worn a ski suit understand
how complicated it is for a
woman to go to the bathroom
when she's wearing a
jumpsuit.

149. Men who are under
five feet six inches tall should
not date fashion models.

Rita Rudner's

150. Even men who consider themselves brave would not want to be in a room alone with Madonna.

151. Men who tie sweaters around their necks and wear loafers with no socks have hot necks and cold ankles.

152. Men who own more than one tuxedo are either in politics, show business, or organized crime.

153. Men who hand out pornographic pamphlets on the street usually don't have balanced diets.

154. Men don't feel the urge to get married as quickly as women do because their clothes all button and zip in the front. Women's dresses usually button and zip in the back. We need men emotionally and sexually, but we also need men to help us get dressed.

Rita Rudner's

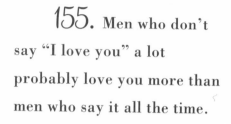

155. Men who don't say "I love you" a lot probably love you more than men who say it all the time.

156. If a man says "I need my space," don't argue with him. Change your phone number. If he goes through the trouble of finding your new phone number, he'll probably need less space.

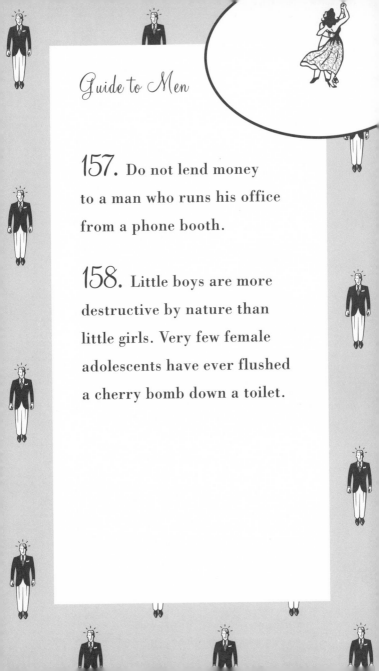

Guide to Men

157. Do not lend money to a man who runs his office from a phone booth.

158. Little boys are more destructive by nature than little girls. Very few female adolescents have ever flushed a cherry bomb down a toilet.

Rita Rudner's

159. Women are more trusting than men. Most men only trust the woman they married, and some don't even trust her.

160. Impulse-buying is not macho. Men rarely call the "Home Shopping Network."

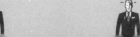

161. Men are self-confident because they grow up identifying with superheroes. Women have bad self-images because they grow up identifying with "Barbie."

162. Men are very confident people. Even a sixty-year-old man with no arms thinks he could play in the Super Bowl if he had to.

163. Men make better burglars than women. Men just show up; women call ahead.

164. Men who play volleyball on the beach aren't worried.

165. Men don't confide in their barbers.

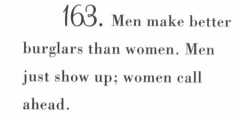

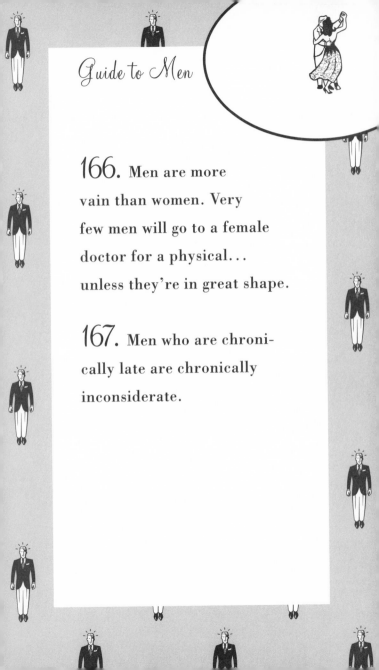

166. Men are more vain than women. Very few men will go to a female doctor for a physical... unless they're in great shape.

167. Men who are chronically late are chronically inconsiderate.

168. Men fantasize about having a harem—a group of women that fulfills all of their wishes. Women don't fantasize about having a male harem; that's just more men to pick up after.

169. A man who goes to the supermarket for a few items would rather walk around the market balancing them than put them in one of those little baskets.

Guide to Men

170. Men aren't as considerate as women. When men are invited to eat dinner at other men's houses, they don't bring anything.

171. Every man in an audience who is picked on by a female comedian dies a little death.

172. Men who stay out late at night and go jogging early in the morning are going to get run over.

173. All men have single socks in their sock drawer that they will never wear and that they will never throw away.

174. Some men are too polite. I was trying to lift weights at the gym and the guy next to me kept saying, "Here, let me get that for you."

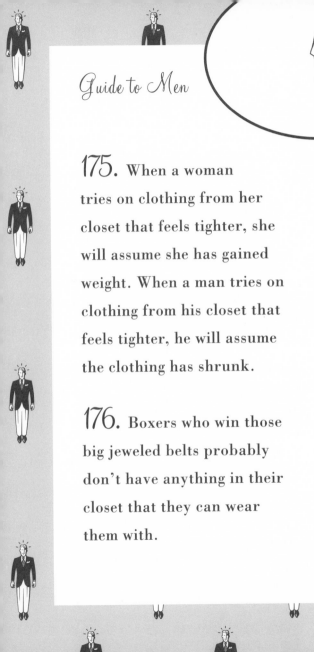

Guide to Men

175. When a woman tries on clothing from her closet that feels tighter, she will assume she has gained weight. When a man tries on clothing from his closet that feels tighter, he will assume the clothing has shrunk.

176. Boxers who win those big jeweled belts probably don't have anything in their closet that they can wear them with.

Rita Rudner's

177. Men over eighty don't care if their clothing matches. The more patterns the better.

178. Men do not need as much bathroom space as women do. My husband shaves in the backyard with a hose.

179. Men who come to your house and bring you wine in a carton are missing the point.

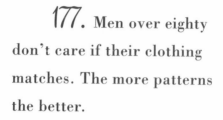

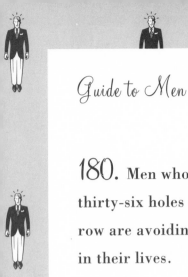

180. Men who play thirty-six holes of golf in a row are avoiding something in their lives.

181. Men get into twice as many car accidents as women, yet all men think they are great drivers.

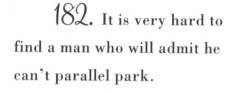

182. It is very hard to find a man who will admit he can't parallel park.

183. Men think they're more important than women because their suit jackets have secret pockets on the inside.

184. Men who are overly affectionate to women in public can't afford a hotel room.

Guide to Men

185. Male menopause is a lot more fun than female menopause. With female menopause you gain weight and get hot flashes. Male menopause—you get to date young girls and drive motor-cycles.

186. All men have mild anxiety attacks when they find themselves in jewelry stores with women.

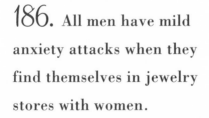

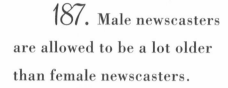

Rita Rudner's

187. Male newscasters are allowed to be a lot older than female newscasters.

188. Amish men will not take you to the movies.

189. Men always have better stereos than women.

190. They also give more thought about where to put their speakers.

191. Men love massages.
Learn to do it. I hired a
masseuse to come to the house
for my husband's birthday.
I thought I was very smart
until the doorbell rang and
I opened the door and there
was an eighteen-year-old
blond girl standing there
saying, "I'm here to give your
husband a massage." I said,
"He's dead."

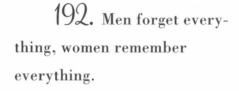

192. Men forget everything, women remember everything.

193. That's why men need instant replays in sports. They've already forgotten what happened.

194. Men would like monogamy better if it sounded less like monotony.

Guide to Men

195. Men over forty
who still do not have
furniture display a distinct
lack of interest in growing up.
I call this "the crate
syndrome." (Exclude men
who have been recently
divorced.)

196. Men love football. I
don't understand all those
men running around franti-
cally bumping into each other
when nothing is even on sale.

197. All men look at Dr. Ruth and wonder how she has gained all that sexual experience.

198. Men who have six or more cats are practicing witchcraft.

199. Men do not think ahead. Men who have tattoos with other women's names on them will always have a great deal of explaining to do when they get undressed.

Guide to Men

200. A man you meet in a hot tub is not a man with whom you will have a long-lasting relationship.

201. The only man who ever had a "little black book" with beautiful women's names in it was Warren Beatty.

202. All the men who read this book will hate it.

About the Author

Rita Rudner is a top concert draw across the United States, entertaining sell-out crowds from Las Vegas to Carnegie Hall. Winner of the 1990 American Comedy Award for Funniest Female Stand-up, she has made numerous appearances on the "Tonight Show" and "Late Night with David Letterman," and in her own comedy specials on HBO and A & E. Rita made her film debut in *Peter's Friends*, which she co-wrote with her husband. She received a 1993 Grammy nomination for the audio version of her first book, *Naked Beneath My Clothes*, a bestseller in both print and audio.